What does it mean to be

Deaf

Louise Spilsbury

Heinemann
LIBRARY

www.heinemann.co.uk/library
Visit our website to find out more information about Heinemann Library books.

To order:
 Phone 44 (0) 1865 888066
 Send a fax to 44 (0) 1865 314091
💻 Visit the Heinemann Bookshop at www.heinemann.co.uk/library to browse our catalogue and order online.

First published in Great Britain by Heinemann Library,
Halley Court, Jordan Hill, Oxford OX2 8EJ,
a division of Reed Educational and Professional Publishing Ltd.
Heinemann is a registered trademark of Reed Educational and Professional Publishing Ltd.

OXFORD MELBOURNE AUCKLAND
JOHANNESBURG BLANTYRE GABORONE
IBADAN PORTSMOUTH (NH) USA CHICAGO

Designed by AMR
Illustrated by Visual Image
Originated by Dot Gradations.
Printed by Wing King Tong, Hong Kong.

ISBN 0 431 13924 5
05 04 03 02 01
10 9 8 7 6 5 4 3 2 1

British Library Cataloguing in Publication Data
Spilsbury, Louise
   What does it mean to be deaf?
   1.Deafness 2.Deaf
   I.Title II.Deaf
   617.8

Acknowledgements
The Publishers would like to thank the following for permission to reproduce photographs:
John Birdsall Photography, p.8; Bubbles/Jennie Woodcock, p.16; Corbis/Anthony Cooper/Ecoscene, p.6; Eye Ubiquitous/Skjod, p.25; Format/Ulrike Preuss, p.4, /Paula Solloway, p.5; Sally & Richard Greenhill, p.24; Impact Photos/Giles Barnard, p.23; Royal National Theatre, p.18; Tony Stone Images/Mary Kate Denny, p.14, /Ian Shaw, p.19; Telegraph Colour Library/Chip Simons, p.9; "Photos courtesy of Teletec International Limited, England", pp. 22, 26; Janine Wiedel, p.17.

The following pictures were taken on commission: Trevor Clifford, p.12, 13, 20, 21, 27. Peter Lake, p.10, 11, 15, 28, 29.

The pictures on the following pages were posed by models who are hearing: 8–11, 15–16, 19, 25, 28–29.

Special thanks to: Benjamin James, Ellie, Jack, Jack Anthony, Lawrence, Madeleine, Nadia, Oscar and Lucia.

With thanks for expert comments from the National Deaf Childrens Society (NDCS). The publishers would also like to thank the Royal National Institute for Deaf People (RNID), and Julie Johnson, PHSE Consultant Writer and Trainer, for their help in the preparation of this book.

Cover photograph reproduced with permission of Janine Wiedel.

Every effort has been made to contact copyright holders of any material reproduced in this book. Any omissions will be rectified in subsequent printings if notice is given to the publishers.

Contents

Any words appearing in the text in bold, **like this**, are explained in the Glossary.

What is deafness?

Deafness is not being able to hear well. If there is a child in your school who is deaf, it means they may not be able to hear some of the sounds around them. They may, for example, be unable to hear teachers talking or friends laughing, or the sound of the bell ringing at the end of playtime.

Some children are born deaf, and others become deaf through illness or some other cause when they are older. There are many different kinds of deafness and many different levels. Young people who are partly deaf may simply have trouble following what people say if there is a lot of noise in the background. A few people are **profoundly** deaf, which means they hear very little.

Ways of communicating

We all need to be able to communicate – to tell other people what we think and how we feel, and to understand what they think and feel. From the moment we are born we start to learn about other people and the world around us by communicating. Of all our five senses – sight, hearing, smell, touch and taste – most of us think of hearing as the most important for keeping in touch with other people.

Being deaf does not mean you cannot do your schoolwork perfectly well. It's just that some people may need extra support.

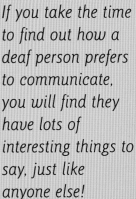
If you take the time to find out how a deaf person prefers to communicate, you will find they have lots of interesting things to say, just like anyone else!

People who are deaf are just as capable of communicating with other people as those who can hear. It is just that they use other ways of talking and listening. They may learn to speak and listen with the help of equipment such as **hearing aids**. These make sounds louder or easier to hear. It may mean they learn to use a language using their hands to sign what they want to say. It does not really matter. After all, what is important about communication is getting across what you want to say, not how you say it.

Facts about deafness

- Around one in seven people is deaf or **hard of hearing**. Fewer than one in ten of these are profoundly deaf.
- About one in four children has glue ear at some time, which causes them to lose some hearing for a while.

How do we hear sounds?

If you twang a ruler or pluck a guitar string, you can see it move backwards and forwards. These movements are called **vibrations**. Any sound, whether it is a soft whisper or the loud honk of a car, makes the air vibrate. These vibrations are called **sound waves**. You cannot see sound waves because they are invisible, but your ears can feel their effects.

When you drop a pebble in a pond, you see ripples spreading outwards. Sound waves are a bit like ripples – they spread out in all directions from the point where they started.

Your ears are not the only part of the body that helps you hear sounds. When you hear things, your ears, part of your **nervous system** and part of your brain are all at work. The outer parts of your ear collect sound waves from the air. When they have done this, they pass them into the short passage just inside your outer ear.

How ears work

Once sound waves are in the ear passage, they travel only a short distance before reaching the **eardrum**. This is like a very thin drum skin stretched across the ear passage. The eardrum is joined to a group of tiny bones, called ossicles, in the middle ear. When sound waves hit the eardrum, they make it vibrate, just like the skin on a real drum. The vibrating eardrum makes the ossicles vibrate too.

The sound waves then move from the ossicles to the **cochlea** inside the inner ear. The cochlea is a coiled-up tube that looks like a snail's shell. It is filled with fluid and tiny hair cells, which are attached to the **auditory nerve**. The auditory nerve carries information about the sound waves from the cochlea to the brain. Then your brain interprets the sound waves and tells you what they are.

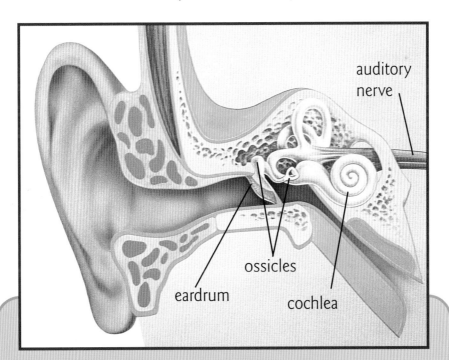

auditory nerve

ossicles

eardrum

cochlea

*Inside your ear, sound vibrations are turned into signals that pass along **nerves** to your brain. Your brain recognizes what the sounds are.*

What causes deafness?

People are deaf because a part of their hearing system does not work. There are lots of different reasons why this happens, causing different kinds and levels of deafness. Often doctors may not be exactly sure why a person is deaf.

Most children and young people are deaf or **hard of hearing** because sound cannot pass through the outer and middle ear to the **cochlea**. This is often because there is something blocking the ear passage, usually fluid in the middle ear (this is called 'glue ear'). This kind of deafness can also be caused by an **infection**. Usually this kind of hearing loss lasts only a short while.

Depending on the cause of a person's deafness, the effects can be temporary or permanent, and the level of hearing loss can vary.

What is glue ear?

Glue ear can cause children up to about the age of eight to lose some of their hearing for a while. About a quarter of all children (one in four) has glue ear at some time. This happens when a sticky fluid (the 'glue') blocks up the middle ear, making it difficult for sounds to get through. Glue ear often happens when someone has a cold, and clears up when the cold is over. If it continues, a doctor can put a little tube into the eardrum to drain off the fluid. This can prevent a build-up of fluid happening again.

Deafness and growing old

The most common cause of deafness is getting old. As people grow older, their chances of becoming deaf or partly deaf greatly increase. In fact, three-quarters of people who are deaf are aged over 60.

Some kinds of deafness happen because the cochlea or the **auditory nerve** does not work properly. Some babies are born with these parts not working properly. Sometimes these parts are damaged later, when children catch illnesses, such as mumps, measles and **meningitis**. Illnesses like these can sometimes lead to deafness.

Accidents can also cause deafness. The ear is very delicate, and a serious injury to the head can damage parts of it. People can also damage their ears by putting things in them, such as fingers or towels, or by listening to very loud noises for too long.

Turn it down! Very loud sounds, such as some machinery or loud music, can damage the ears and cause deafness. If you use a personal stereo try not to turn the volume up too high.

Testing for deafness

It is important that children who are deaf are **diagnosed** as early as possible. Once they are diagnosed, they can get the help they need to learn to communicate. Hearing is especially important because, as a baby grows into a child, listening to people is usually the way they learn most of all – until they learn to read and write.

In some countries, hearing is tested as soon as a baby is born. In other places, a baby may only be tested if there were difficulties during the birth or if the baby was born very early and is quite small. Hearing tests are also done when babies and young children have their standard health check-ups. Doctors or health visitors do simple checks at first. Then, if they spot a problem, they send the child to see a **specialist**.

It is possible to test the hearing of babies as young as one day old. It does not bother them. Some babies even sleep through the test!

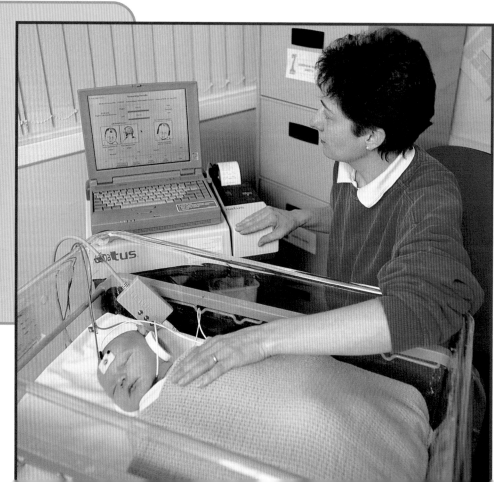

Other hearing tests

When an older child goes to the doctor because they are worried about their hearing, the doctor first talks about when and how they find it difficult to hear. For example, is it hard to hear anything at all, or do they catch just snatches of conversation in a noisy classroom? Doctors also ask if there is anything that might have caused the problem, such as a recent illness. Then they check the ears to see if there is a blockage. If there is not, and the doctor feels there may be another reason for the hearing difficulties, the child may be sent to see an **audiologist**.

An audiologist carries out hearing tests. There are a number of different tests for measuring hearing. The audiologist decides which test to use, depending on the age of the person and the kind of hearing loss they are being tested for. The results of the tests are often marked on an **audiogram**. This is a chart that shows what sounds a child can hear and how loud a sound has to be before they can hear it.

This boy is having his hearing tested. The machine bleeps at different levels of loudness so the audiologist can find out which sounds he can hear.

Meet Lani, Lucia and Oscar

My name is Lani and I'm Oscar's mum. Oscar was born severely deaf in both his ears. Doctors spotted this when he was sixteen months old. Oscar was fitted with **hearing aids** immediately.

This was when the hard work started for Oscar, and indeed all of us. Oscar was suddenly bombarded with all the noises of the world around him, after knowing only silence. He was confused and angry. He hated wearing his hearing aids and was always pulling them out. He threw them down the toilet, out of the car window, and even posted them through neighbours' letterboxes! We gradually encouraged him to wear them so that he could hear what other people said and so learn to speak himself.

Oscar is now four and a half. For the past two years we have been encouraging him to listen and helping him to make sense of different sounds. He understands and recognizes most sounds now. He jokes and squabbles with his brothers and sisters, loves listening to stories, asks endless questions and even talks in his sleep!

Hi. My name is Lucia. I'm Oscar's big sister and I'm nine years old. I don't really think of Oscar as being deaf, he's just Oscar. He goes to an ordinary school, just like me. The only difference is that he has some help from teachers who have special training in working with deaf children. He's happy at school and he has lots of friends there.

I suppose there are certain things that I'm used to doing because he's deaf, which I don't really think about any more. Like, if it's noisy, I have to look at his face when I talk to him so he can read my lips. And I always talk to him normally. If you try too hard to make words louder, you end up with your mouth wide open and it makes it hard for him to work out what you're saying. I've learnt not to get fed up when he doesn't understand. Sometimes you just have to say things a few times over.

Oscar likes me to play games with him a lot.

Being deaf

Every young person adapts to their deafness in different ways. They may do what they can to make the most of what hearing they have. Very few deaf people can hear no sounds whatsoever. An operation can help some deaf children to hear better. Many others wear **hearing aids** – devices that make sounds louder or easier to hear.

Some deaf children learn to communicate in the same way most people do – by spending time talking with other people. Some children learn to speak with the help of different kinds of equipment and teaching. Other children may prefer to use **sign language** and **finger spelling** to communicate. In finger spelling the fingers are used to spell out words or names. Many people also **lip-read**. They watch the shapes that people's mouths make as they speak to work out what they are saying. This is tricky – it often involves a lot of guesswork. Lots of young people choose to use one or a combination of these methods.

This woman is using sign language to talk about the book the children are looking at.

Communication tips

If there is someone at your school or in your family who lip-reads or uses a hearing aid, there are ways you can help.

- Before you start talking, make sure you have their attention. Make sure they can see your lips properly, too.
- Try to talk in a place that is not too noisy, away from the main playground, for example.
- Don't shout. This doesn't help, because shouting changes the way you move your mouth when you say words. This makes it hard for a lip-reader to follow. It can also make you look angry even though you are not.
- Speak clearly, but not slowly. If you slow down your speech, you may change the way you move your mouth when you say words.
- Try to talk normally. Don't forget, we all understand part of what other people are saying by their facial expressions and their body movements.

(See page 18 for information about sign languages)

Some words may be difficult to hear or lip-read. No problem – just keep a pad and pen handy and write down anything that is tricky, such as an unusual name.

Hearing aids

There are several different kinds of **hearing aids**, but they all do basically the same job – they **amplify** sounds. This means they make sounds louder and make it easier for children to know what is going on around them. Hearing aids don't give people who are deaf perfect hearing, and they are not suitable for everyone. They also make all sounds louder, not just the ones you want to hear. In a classroom, this means that a child can hear not only the teacher's voice, but also the distracting sounds of other children.

Hearing aids have a **microphone**, an **amplifier** and a receiver, which is a tiny loudspeaker. Hearing aids are powered by tiny batteries. They pick up sound signals through the tiny microphone, and the amplifier makes them louder. The amount of amplification people need depends on the kind and level of deafness they have. Most hearing aids have a volume control switch, so the people wearing them can make the sound louder or quieter.

Most people find that their hearing aids work best when they are in quiet surroundings. It is easier to hear what other people are saying without background noise such as traffic or lots of people talking.

The kind of hearing aid a person uses depends on the kind of deafness they have. Most hearing aids are worn behind the ear. These are in two parts. The part behind the ear holds the battery, the microphone and the amplifier. The second part, called the ear mould, fits inside the ear. It is connected to the first part by a tube. Some hearing aids have everything in one piece that fits snugly in the person's ear.

A hearing aid has two parts. One part is worn behind the ear. The other part fits inside the ear

Cochlear implants

Some people who are **profoundly** deaf because of a damaged **cochlea** have a hearing aid called a **cochlear implant**. Part of the aid is worn on the outside of the body and part of the aid is put into the ear during an operation. The outside part of the aid changes sounds into electrical signals. These electrical signals are sent to the inside part of the aid and from there to the brain.

Cochlear implants give only a sensation of hearing. Children who have them need lots of help learning what different sounds mean. Many profoundly deaf people choose one of the many other options open to them.

Sign language

It does not matter which language a person speaks, so long as they can communicate with other people. Many young people who are deaf learn a language that uses the hands, the face and the upper part of the body to communicate. This is called **sign language**. Sign languages are completely different from the spoken language of a country. They have their own grammar and word order. Different countries use different sign languages. Even though countries like the UK and the USA use the same spoken language, they have different sign languages.

At this theatre performance hearing people are signing the words the actors are saying.

Sign languages across the world

- British Sign Language (BSL) is the most frequently used sign language in Britain. BSL is used by about 70,000 people. It has its own grammar and word order that are not the same as spoken English.
- American Sign Language (ASL) is used by more than half a million deaf people in the USA.
- The sign language of Australia's deaf community is called Auslan.
- There are special international signs used at meetings of deaf people from different countries across the world.

Using sign language

When we talk we don't just use words to tell people what we mean. We show how we feel with body language – the way we move parts of our body when we speak – and our facial expressions. This is the same for sign language, too. For example, the difference between two similar sentences like 'Did you give me a drink?' and 'I gave you a drink' is shown both by the hand signs used and the direction in which those signs are made. If someone asks 'Did you give me a drink?' they signal from the other person to themself, and they raise their eyebrows at the end of the sentence to show they are asking a question. Think about what gestures you make when you speak. You will probably find that you often do many of these kinds of things without really thinking.

Sign language is a language like any other. People can say something in sign language as quickly (if not quicker) as they can using spoken words. You can argue in sign, discuss mathematical problems, or share a good joke.

Meet Ghazala and Nadia

My name is Ghazala and I am Nadia's mum. Nadia is eight years old. When she was about three months old I noticed that she did not turn her head when I called her. She didn't seem to respond to very loud noises either, and would just go on sleeping, whatever was going on around her. By the time she was seven months old, and after many tests, we were told that Nadia is **profoundly** deaf in both ears.

She was fitted with **hearing aids** straightaway. At first, special teachers tried to help her learn to speak and listen. But she found she got on better with **sign language**. So then we all began to use sign language – Nadia, her dad and I, and her two brothers. Nadia is very happy using sign language and she is very good at **finger spelling** too. She is also learning how to **lip-read**.

Nadia goes to a school for children who are deaf. Her teachers speak and use sign language at the same time so she can understand everything they say. Nadia enjoys school and she is very good at drawing and writing.

Hello. My name is Nadia. I'm deaf and I go to a school with other children who are deaf. I like my school. My favourite subjects are art and maths. I especially like drawing people. I enjoy spelling as well. I'm not so keen on outdoor sports, though last year I tried riding and swimming, and I play outside with my brothers in summer.

My brothers are older than me. Their names are Khuram and Muzaffar. We enjoy playing snooker together and we like bowling too. I play games on the Play Station with Muzaffar. I also like watching television, especially my videos. My favourite ones are *Friends* and I also like *Tarzan*.

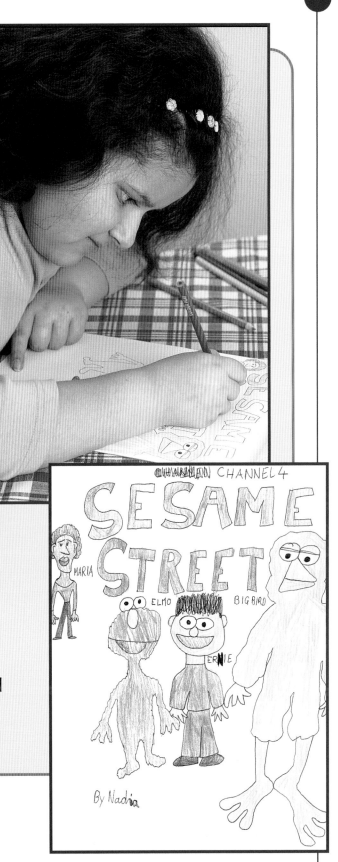

Living with deafness

There are lots of things in our everyday lives that can provide challenges for deaf people. These range from using the telephone or watching television to listening to teachers when they explain a new idea.

There are many devices that help young people who are deaf to overcome practical difficulties like these. For example, you may be surprised to know that many deaf people use the telephone every day. Some use telephones that have a volume control to make the sound louder. Others have special devices in the earpiece of the phone (the part you hold to your ear) that can be used with **hearing aids**. These devices help deaf people hear voices on a phone more clearly.

Many deaf people use text telephones. These have a small keyboard to type messages that come up on a single-line screen. You place a normal telephone handset on to a special receiver and dial the telephone number as usual. With a text telephone you can receive messages and type replies back instantly.

It is easy to chat to friends on a text telephone. These special telephones may cost no more to use than ordinary phones.

Photo courtesy of Teletec International Limited, England.

How does it feel?

There are lots of devices deaf people can use to help in practical ways, but how does it feel to be deaf? Some young people who are deaf say they have times when it gets them down. They may feel cut off from other people or they may resent having to wear hearing aids or use special equipment. People who are deaf are also sometimes teased at school or treated as if they were different.

*Some groups for young people who are deaf organize holidays. At this activity centre the instructor is using **sign language** to teach a group how to canoe.*

Most people who are deaf say that being deaf is just a small part of who they are. They can do all or nearly all the things other people can do – and just as well. Most of the time, young people who are deaf just get on with living their life. As well as making friends at school or home, they may join clubs or groups to meet other young people who are deaf. Many deaf children are proud to be deaf and enjoy being part of the deaf community.

At school

The kind of school a young person who is deaf goes to depends on what suits them best. Some children prefer to go to schools that are for deaf children only. Many others go to ordinary schools. Some rely on **hearing aids** or equipment such as **radio aids** to allow them to attend classes alongside children who can hear. They may have some extra help, perhaps with their speech, from specially trained teachers who come to the school. Some have their lessons with other deaf children in special classrooms that are part of an ordinary school. Although they have many lessons separately, they usually have some lessons with hearing children and join in with activities such as school trips and assemblies.

Radio aids

If a deaf child goes to school with children who can hear, they may use radio aid systems to help them join in lessons. The teacher wears a special microphone that relays what they are saying directly to a receiver connected to child's hearing aid. This means the child can hear wherever they sit in class. These aids are small and easy to swap over when a different teacher takes over the lesson.

Making friends

Most children who are deaf go to ordinary schools alongside children who can hear. They say they prefer it because they like being with different kinds of people and they get to make friends with people who live near home.

One problem for deaf children who go to a school where most people can hear is that they may get teased or bullied. They may not like wearing their hearing aids because these often show and this may make them feel different. They may also get picked on because their voices sound different when they speak. No one should put up with bullying. If this happens to you, or you see someone else being bullied, tell a teacher so they can sort it out.

Sports activities are a great way for deaf and hearing children to work and play together. After all, you don't have to be able to hear to score a winning goal!

Most children who have hearing difficulties just want to be accepted for who they are. They get on with making their own friends, doing their schoolwork and all of the other things they enjoy.

At home

Some people who are deaf have a few gadgets to help them at home, so they can take care of themselves. For example, some people have extra-loud doorbells, so they know when someone is at the door. Lots of families have a doorbell connected up to a lamp in their child's room – or even all the lights in the house – so that they flash on and off when someone rings the doorbell.

A smoke alarm is another household device that usually relies on sound. It gives off loud beeping noises when it detects smoke to warn people there may be a fire. It is vital that everyone knows when one goes off. Smoke alarms can be wired up to the lights so they flash while the smoke alarm beeps. They can even be connected to a pad under a child's pillow that **vibrates** (moves backwards and forwards) to wake them up.

Some young people who are deaf use special alarm clocks. Some have flashing lights, and a pad under their pillow that vibrates when it's time to get up. People who wear **hearing aids** usually take them out at night, so a clock like this is a must if they want to get to school on time!

Photo courtesy of Teletec International Limited, England.

Watching TV

If someone is deaf, there are lots of ways they can enjoy watching television, too. Some deaf children wear personal listening aids. These are about the size of a personal stereo. The listening aid usually uses a small **microphone** on a speaker on the television. The **amplified** sound goes to headphones or the child's hearing aid.

Many homes have special Teletext or Ceefax television sets. These have lots of different screen pages that show written information, like football results or news reports. There are also some programmes for deaf people with presenters who use **sign language**.

Many films and programmes on television or video can also be watched with subtitles. Subtitles are words that run along the bottom of the screen. The words are not always the exact written form of what is being said on the screen, because these may take up too much space. Sometimes they are a summary – a shorter version. It can be tricky to watch what is going on and read the subtitles at the same time, but most people enjoy it once they get the hang of it.

Many young people who are deaf enjoy watching films with subtitles.

- Madeline, where's your pad?
- I left it in the other gallery.

Meet Jonathan

My name is Jonathan. I go to a school where some kids are deaf and some can hear. I have most of my classes with people who are deaf like me. Then we meet up with the others at playtimes and lunchtimes, and for sports lessons and assemblies. I wear two **hearing aids**, and at

school my teacher also uses a **radio aid**. I can speak and **lip-read**, but that can be tricky and it's pretty tiring, so when I'm with friends who are deaf we often use **sign language** to talk to each other.

My best friends are in my class and they are deaf like me. But I've got other friends in school, too. No one here makes a thing about us being deaf. We all just get on with it. Some of the hearing kids say they think they're lucky to have deaf kids at their school. They say they used to feel awkward when they met a deaf person, but now they know we're just like anyone else! We use computers a lot at school. Me and my friend Max work on lots of our projects on a computer together.

As well as using computers at school, I've got my own at home. I think the Internet is really great for everyone, but it's especially useful for deaf people like me. I can log on and find out loads of information that it was hard to get hold of before. I can also use e-mail to chat to my friends.

I joined a club for young deaf people last year. I joined because a friend of mine told me they were going on a rock-climbing holiday and I liked the sound of it. I went on the holiday and it was really cool. We get together once a fortnight, just to hang out and talk about stuff. I like getting together with my friends who are deaf. We also organize trips or holidays together. This year we're planning a skiing holiday. The instructors will be using sign language to tell us what to do. I can't wait.

Glossary

amplifier machine that makes sounds louder

amplify make louder

audiogram graph that shows the level of a person's hearing loss (how much difficulty they have in hearing)

audiologist person who gives hearing tests and who fits hearing aids

auditory nerve nerve that carries information about sounds from the cochlea to the brain

cochlea the part of the inner ear that looks like a snail shell. It changes sound waves into signals that travel along the auditory nerve to the brain.

cochlear implant device which changes sounds into electrical signals and sends them to the inner ear.

diagnose when a doctor decides what disease or condition a person has

eardrum circular piece of skin (like a drum skin) that separates the outer ear from the middle ear. It turns sounds into vibrations.

finger spelling used as part of sign language, to spell out words or names

hard of hearing when someone finds it difficult to hear some sounds

hearing aid device that amplifies sounds (makes them louder)

infection disease in the body or part of the body

lip-read when people can tell what someone is saying by watching the way their mouth moves when they speak

meningitis serious illness where germs attack the lining of the brain, and which can damage a person's hearing system (inner ear and auditory nerve)

microphone piece of equipment that collects sounds and sends them out through a hearing aid or amplifier

nerves parts of the body that look like pieces of string that take messages to and from the brain with information from our five senses (sight, taste, touch, hearing and smell)

nervous system the body's network of nerves

profoundly when this word refers to a level of deafness it means near total deafness. Very few deaf people have no hearing at all.

radio aid device worn by a teacher, which relays (passes) his or her voice directly into a deaf child's hearing aid

sign language language in which people use their hands, upper part of the body, facial expressions, and gestures to communicate

sound wave the way sounds move in the air

specialist doctor who has done extra training in one 'special' subject, like hearing difficulties

vibrate/vibration move backwards and forwards quickly. When you twang a ruler or an elastic band you can see the vibrations.

Helpful books and addresses

BOOKS
Senses: Hearing, Karen Hartley, Chris Macro and Philip Taylor, Heinemann Library, 2000

When It's Hard to Hear, Judith Condon, Franklin Watts, 1998

Think About Being Deaf, Maggie Woolley, Belitha Press, 1998

Living with Deafness, Emma Haughton, Hodder Wayland, 1999.

ORGANIZATIONS AND WEBSITES
The National Deaf Children's Society, (NDCS)
15 Dufferin Street
London EC1Y 8UR
Information and Helpline:
020 7250 0123 (voice and text telephone number)
Fax: 020 7251 5020
E-mail: helpline@ndcs.org.uk
website: www.ndcs.org.uk

This society provides information, advice and support to all families with deaf children and to young deaf people.

The British Deaf Association
1–3 Worship Street
London EC2A 2AB
Tel: 020 7588 3520
website: www.bda.org.uk

Royal National Institute for Deaf People (RNID)
19–23 Featherstone Street
London EC1Y 8SL
Helpline: 0870 605 0123
website: rnid.org.uk

Deafblind UK
100 Bridge Street
Peterborough PE1 1DY
Tel: 01733 358100
website: www.deafblind.org.uk
This organization provides support for those who are deaf and blind.

IN AUSTRALIA
Australian Association of the Deaf
Level 6
225 Clarence Street
Sydney NSW 2000
Tel: 02 9262 3506
Fax: 02 9262 3508
E-mail: aad@fl.net.au

Index

Titles in the *What does it mean to have/be* series include:

Hardback   0 431 13924 5

Hardback   0 431 13921 0

Hardback   0 431 13920 2

Hardback   0 431 13922 9

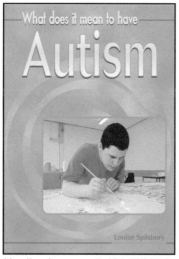

Hardback   0 431 13925 3

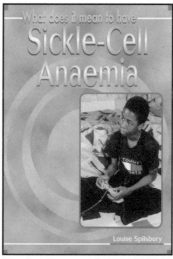

Hardback   0 431 13923 7

Find out about the other titles in this series on our website www.heinemann.co.uk/library